Robert Bigsby

National Honours and Their Noblest Claimants

Robert Bigsby

National Honours and Their Noblest Claimants

ISBN/EAN: 9783337191818

Printed in Europe, USA, Canada, Australia, Japan

Cover: Foto ©ninafisch / pixelio.de

More available books at **www.hansebooks.com**

NATIONAL HONOURS

AND

THEIR NOBLEST CLAIMANTS.

" Men of high merit stamp a right to honour with the seal of reflected eminence."
Anon.

" The chief glory of every people arises from its authors."
Dr. Samuel Johnson.

BY

ROBERT BIGSBY, LL.D.,

K.J.S. OF PORTUGAL, ETC. ETC.,

Member of the Intrepidi, Pellegrini, Olimpica, Daphnica, Gioenia, and Cosentina
Academies, and Honorary Director of the Royal Academy of Palermo.

LONDON:

PRINTED BY J. E. TAYLOR & CO., LITTLE QUEEN STREET,
LINCOLN'S INN FIELDS.

1867.

INSCRIBED

AS A

TRIBUTE OF GRATITUDE

TO THE MEMORY OF

THE RIGHT HONOURABLE

HENRY JOHN TEMPLE,

VISCOUNT PALMERSTON, K.G.,

G.C.B., G.C.T.S. OF PORTUGAL, ETC. ETC. ETC. ETC.,

LATE PREMIER OF ENGLAND,

TO WHOSE RECOMMENDATION TO THE SOVEREIGN I OWE
THE FLATTERING DISTINCTION OF
A NATIONAL RECOGNITION OF MY HUMBLE LITERARY SERVICES,*
A FAVOUR RENDERED MORE ESTIMABLE BY THE
EXTREME COURTESY AND CORDIALITY
ACCOMPANYING ITS BESTOWAL, AND THE REMEMBRANCE OF
WHICH MUST EVER BE THE MORE GRATIFYING
AS RECALLING THE APPROBATION OF A TRULY GREAT MAN,
WHOSE LONG CAREER OF PUBLIC HONOUR CLAIMS ONE OF THE
NOBLEST VOLUMES IN THE ANNALS OF HIS COUNTRY;
WHOSE NAME WAS A CHARM THAT STRENGTHENED THE CAUSE
OF LIBERAL GOVERNMENT THROUGHOUT THE WORLD,
WHILE IT AWOKE THE BITTEREST HATRED OF DESPOTIC CABINETS;
WHO, WHILE HE MADE ENGLAND RESPECTED
BY HER FOREIGN ENEMIES, TRIUMPHED EQUALLY OVER THE
BAFFLED ENMITY OF HER DOMESTIC FOES; AND
WHO, HAVING BEQUEATHED TO SUCCEEDING STATESMEN
A BRILLIANT EXAMPLE
OF SAGACITY, PATRIOTIC SPIRIT, AND INDOMITABLE COURAGE
(THE THREE HIGHEST QUALITIES OF GENUINE RULERSHIP),
DIED, IN THE ZENITH OF HIS FAME,
LEAVING A MEMORY THAT WILL EVER BE FRESH AND GREEN IN
THE HEARTS OF THE BRITISH PEOPLE.

ROBERT BIGSBY.

* Civil List Pension.

PREFACE.

It has ever been seen that the exclusion of men
of letters from a just share in the distribution
of national honours has no tendency to weaken
the attraction of a literary life in this country.
Though coronets and mitres, governorships and
embassies, privy-councillorships, baronetcies, and
knighthoods, have been copiously allotted to
men of inferior ability or of no ability at all,
while personal obscurity, attended with various
degrees of poverty, has been the almost certain
condition of others upon whom the Almighty
has showered his choicest gifts, those which

elevate and adorn the nature of Man as an intellectual being, and who have cherished, enriched, enlarged, and perfected those gifts by unceasing meditation and devoted study,—we yet find that the prevailing sense of what was due to their fellow-creatures, as the beneficiaries of this high trust, has constrained them to engage such privileged faculties in the one great object of supporting the "dignity and honour" of their country by the application of those stores of genius and knowledge to the noble cause of literature, thereby cheerfully incurring the penalty of social martyrdom, and burying every personal prospect in unmitigated ruin. Obscurity and poverty, as opposed to high place and a corresponding state of dignified independence, has been the almost unfailing result of a dedication of the loftiest talents to this the most elevated pursuit of human ambition. England has hitherto been content that such Virtue, in accordance with ZENO's axiom, should be "its own reward." In other countries, poorer and *reputed as less civilized than our own,* we see a juster sense of acknowledgment prevail, and while men of letters find their talents employed in the highest branches of the public service, the most distinguished national honours await them. It is just that those who are rich should be the most generous, and England, as the wealthiest country on the globe, ought not to be the most negligent of the claims upon her generosity or gratitude.

Literary men have seldom made public their privations and sorrows. They have lived on, year after year, in unobserved misery, submitting with quiet resignation to their wretched lot; and I am prepared to expect that this effort of mine to bring the condition of such uncomplaining sufferers under the notice of those who have the power to assist unbefriended merit, will give pain and annoyance, as tending to lower in social opinion the estimation they possess as a class. Should this be the case, I can only remark that my hope of success in raising a powerful sympathy in their favour, in the breasts of all good men, and, as an approximate result, of driving away the ghost of penury from their path of hopeless endurance, will counterbalance the objections entertained towards my design.

Amongst many other instances of distress, I remember that of a man for whom I felt a sincere and warm friendship—a tender and reverent regard. A nobler, gentler nature, a more refined and elevated taste, a more masterly attainment of literary skill and learning, associated with a poetical genius of commanding power, has seldom existed. That man died an early victim to the galling yoke of forced exertion inflicted upon him by his literary taskmasters. I had, on rare occasions, the privilege of hearing him read with a poet's enthusiasm the pages of a work destined, as I believe, to have achieved for its author an enduring and glorious name on the roll of Fame —a work prosecuted by him at distant and uncertain intervals, at moments of the briefest leisure, through the overruling necessity of devoting his almost uninterrupted attention to those loath-

some acts of drudgery so unfitted for the scope
of his natural inclinations and peculiar attainments,—a necessity rendered still more impe-
rious by the dependence of a sick wife and infant
family, whom his unsparing devotedness to this
course of labour hardly preserved from the hor-
rors of threatened destitution. His death was
the direct result of an overtaxed brain, bewil-
dered, as it had long been, by the pressure of
demands unfitted for the exercise of his literary
genius. Under such heart-wearing toil, long-
continued confinement, harassing anxieties, and
pressing privations—telling as they did against
a feeble physical constitution—what wonder that
his energies gave way, and that his daily task-
work became impeded, while, with the pride of a
lofty nature, he forbore, till it was too late, to
communicate those pecuniary embarrassments
which quickly followed! I spare the reader the
sequel of his fate. Not a line of that splendid
poem which had been the pride of his heart was
suffered to survive him. Memories of this kind

have hovered over my desk while I committed my thoughts to the following pages. May they not have been written in vain !

I believe that the instances are few in which men of literary merit are selected for employment in any department of our public service. They are compelled to depend on their unassisted exertions, as authors, for the requirements of each passing day. This necessity would be far less regrettable, if it were happily allowed them to select according to their several abilities the work they were necessitated to perform; but it almost invariably happens that the subjects for composition are chosen for them by the publisher, whose immediate market for such literary wares is the only matter consulted; and it follows, as a too general result, that books are compiled in a listless and inefficient manner, furnished at a given price, within a given period, with little regard to their quality or intrinsic value. But give the same writers leave to choose their own subjects, and allow them ample time for the accumulation and arrangement of their materials, and how wide would be the difference in the style and treatment observable in their productions! I say, then, if, as is indisputable, the public look to this class of men as guides in every direction of human knowledge, as the cultivators of the national taste and morals, as the best guardians of the liberties of the commonwealth,—in a word, as the great promoters of civilization throughout the wide family of mankind, —it follows that it is a matter of policy—to say nothing of justice—to enable such men to pursue their labours for the public good on such terms as are consistent with the free execution of their severally chosen undertakings. Rescue them from the slavery they now endure, by the grant of a literary pension, or a befitting stipend for the discharge of occasional duties in one or other of the public branches of service, and *from such patronage would spring fruit a hundredfold in the gathering.* I cannot conceive the case of a greater sufferer than that of the man who, with strong yearnings for the liberty of adapting his peculiar powers to a task of literary exertion congenial with the character or special bent of his genius, must bow to the ignoble necessity of accepting such mean drudgery for his pen as is afforded under the slave-compelling dictation of speculative traders dealing in books as mere articles of merchandise. Such terms are in themselves revolting to any man of intellect and integrity. He loses self-respect in submitting to them.

Need I say more to enlist the sympathy of any reader, whose judgment would be worthy of regard ?

NATIONAL HONOURS

AND THEIR

NOBLEST CLAIMANTS.

———◆———

"It is by most persons acknowledged, that no maxim in politics is more indisputable than that a nation should have many honours to bestow on those who perform national services. Honorary distinctions excite emulation, cherish public spirit, and create an ambition highly conducive to the good of the country."
—*Dr. Nicholas Carlisle.*

VIRTUE, by which is meant not moral excellence alone, but also the spirit and energy that attain superiority in the nobler pursuits of life, is, or ought to be, an unfailing passport to HONOUR. We use the word HONOUR in the sense of a recognition from the State, through the grant of an honorary distinction from its chief ruler.

The Athenians raised a noble statue to the memory of Æsop, and placed a slave on a pedes-

B

tal, that men might know the way to HONOUR *was open to* ALL.

All virtues were made deities by the Romans. MARCELLUS erected two temples, one to VIRTUE, the other to HONOUR. They were built in such a manner, that to see the Temple of HONOUR it was necessary to pass through that of VIRTUE ;— a happy allegory, deserving alike the deepest consideration of sovereigns and their subjects. The duties of subjects are closely defined; those of monarchs are less distinctly mapped out. Let us hear what an author of modern times says of the duty of rulers; and the remark is of value, as proceeding from a writer distinguished by the united recommendations of keen discernment and candid utterance :—" It is expected that they who are high and eminent in the State shall not only provide for its necessary safety and subsistence, but omit nothing which may contribute to its dignity and honour." What, we ask, can more powerfully contribute to the " dignity and honour" of a State than the adoption of a system of assured rewards for those who justly merit them ?

Assuming an answer in the affirmative, we propose a second question, Who are the *chief benefactors* of a nation, and to whom is the world at large most deeply indebted ?

Dr. Johnson, the great moralist, has said that the "*chief glory* of every people arises from its AU-THORS." "The beneficial influence of literature," observes the elder D'Israeli, " is felt through successive ages; and they, indeed, are the *chief benefactors* of mankind, who bestow on posterity their most refined pleasures and their most useful speculations."

" The *great benefactors* of mankind," remarks the brilliant contributor of an unacknowledged essay in one of our older magazines, to whose pages we regret our present inability to refer, " are they who teach men to be wise, virtuous, and happy. They are the heralds of heaven—the messengers of peace on earth, and goodwill towards man. Their voice is the voice of VIRTUE, and its echo is GLORY."

Anaxagoras, the Clazomenian philosopher, used to say he preferred a *grain of wisdom* to *heaps of gold*. Socrates, Euripides, and Pericles were in the number of his pupils. The latter often consulted him on matters of State.

" It is *mind* that makes the MAN." Of all claims to human distinction, those founded on superiority of genius and intellectual attainments, if accompanied by a corresponding elevation of virtuous sentiment, are most worthy of esteem.

Having clearly ascertained what class of men are the *chief glory* of a nation, and regarding as equally obvious and incontrovertible the fact that it is the duty of those who rule to neglect nothing that can contribute to the "dignity and honour" of a State, we are morally entitled to demand a just and unequivocal answer, from those who govern, to the suggested query, Why are our most eminent literary worthies not regarded in the light of "*public servants*," and, as such, allowed to participate in the distribution of "*State rewards*"?

It has been said that men in power prefer to bestow benefits upon the undeserving, because in such instances they *grant a favour;* while, in conferring honour or advantage upon those who merit it, they only *discharge a debt.* They ought, however, to remember that when they reward the deserving they pay a high compliment to themselves, by showing that they possess the superior qualities of mind which induce an appreciation of the juster claim of MERIT. Doing justice to worthy qualities is a credit to our judgment. No obligation can be of more force than to render to eminent VIRTUE its due rewards.

Good, learned, and *happy* are epithets which should never be dissociated. A barbarous state of society wills otherwise. The *"Abderita mens"* has too long prevailed on this question. Let us shake off our sluggish disposition and stupidity, and show that the air we breathe is wholesome, and favourable to greater activity and strength of mental resolve. Let us learn to do honour to such as have "deserved well of society, and laid out worthy and manly qualities in the service of the public." The public always reap greater advantage from the example of successful MERIT than the deserving man himself can possibly be possessed of. Yet how rare an occurrence is that of a due reward assigned by his country to a man of conspicuous desert!

"Nothing," says GRANGER, "could form a more curious collection of memoirs than ANECDOTES OF PREFERMENT. Could the secret history of great men be traced, it would appear that MERIT is rarely the first step to advancement. It would much oftener be found to be owing to superficial qualifications, and even vices."

The records of history, and the observation of experience, alike teach us that MERIT often fails to meet with its just acknowledgment. The opinion of society seems to suggest that poverty and obscurity are the fitting conditions of the poet and the philosopher. True it is, that wealth and power are rarely the acquisitions of wisdom and virtue. It is a vulgar axiom that "fools have fortune." It may be that the world is sometimes jealous of the most deserving, or that it has not yet discovered who are our nation's noblest worthies—its loftiest heroes, its most meritorious citizens.

"The world," says Dr. KNOX, "has seldom been grateful to its *benefactors*. It has neglected, banished, poisoned, and crucified them."

"The eighteenth century," remarks Dr. JORTIN, a former archdeacon of London, and a writer of superior talent, "has been in our country an age of public charities; but one charity is still wanting; and that is, an *Hospital for Scholars*." Again he observes :—" Scholars have a poor time of it in every country; in ours especially, where all they can get by their abilities, industry, and reputation, is just to keep their heads above water."

They are admired and neglected, praised and starved.

A writer of great merit, in the last century, speaking of a piece of preferment he expected to receive, but of which he was disappointed, says— " A person who is not worth the naming was preferred to me, by the solicitation of—*it matters*

not who." Another project of advancement having also failed, he adds, in reference to the cause,
that it was attributable to the "opposition of—
it matters not who." "This *it matters not who,"*
he observes, "is often a very troublesome gentle-
man to persons of merit, and a very sedulous
besetter of great persons."

To birth is conceded the preferment which
belongs justly to MERIT. "Non idem licet nobis,"
to borrow the words of CICERO, "quod iis qui
nobili genere nati sunt; quibus omnia, dormi-
entibus, deferuntur."

How often have we seen a beggarly pittance,
counted as with an eye to pence and shillings,
accorded to the highly-deserving man of letters,
while to the insignificant but influentially-con-
nected hanger-on of some official department a
munificent provision has been extended! How
often have we seen the highest honours of the
State awarded to those whose claims could not
be exposed with decent gravity to the scarcely
awakened discernment of some youthful ques-
tioner! How often have we seen coronets and
baronetcies bestowed as the reward of unconsti-
tutional services, or given, as "pearls cast before
swine," in mere sordid deference to men with no
other recommendation than that ascribed to the

length of their rent-roll, or the extent of their
cash investments. *Grubs* and *caterpillars*, merely
born, as HORACE expresses it, "consumere
fruges," are such claimants for unenviable no-
toriety,—born to consume the fruits of the earth,
and for no other end, as it would seem, than that
of becoming the unworthy recipients of such
degraded dignities.

"Titles of honour conferred upon such as have
no personal MERIT to deserve them," says TACITUS,
"are at best but the royal stamp set upon base
metal."

What then must be the feelings of men of
honourable sentiments, when, after a life of prolonged sacrifice for the elevation of their country's
literary repute, they find themselves neglected
by the hand of power,—nay, see the favours of
royalty reserved for what are called "*State services*," as if any higher *services* could be rendered
to the *State* than those they have themselves
rendered? Yes, what must be their sense of
such base injustice when they contemplate the
scanty material resources which, in the enthusiasm of their disinterested zeal, they had looked
to as sufficient for the decent sustenance of de-
clining years in that period of life which they had
hoped to see cheered by the enlivening beams of

a publicly expressed national sympathy, as testified in a recognition from the State, in reward of their long public services?

When, we ask, shall we see the glittering star and the shining *cordon* conceded, in this country, to the breast of him who has enshrined his name in the title-page of some glorious epic, or who has poured forth his celestially-inspired thoughts in an impassioned series of lyrical triumphs, or high dramatic achievements? When shall we witness the gift of high place or munificent pension to the deserving man of letters who has devoted the "midnight oil" and the *noontide ray* to protracted toil—toil whose intensity would cause to shrink from it the coarsest natures inured to manual labour, could they gain an adequate idea of the exhaustive strain upon the mental powers which that exertion involved? The fact undeniably is, that men of this heroic stamp—men thirsting for the lofty prize of immortality awarded to genius—are looked upon in official circles in a contemptuous light. They are regarded as blind and misguided creatures—energetic triflers — vain seekers of an empty name, which they hope to bequeath, as a sacred record, to the care of a distant posterity—visionaries insanely in love with the allegorized impersonation of FAME, a goddess whose vaunted *golden* trumpet is the only *gold* in her possession, and whose sole function it is to bestow on her fondest admirers *an empty blast!* While such opinions are more or less strongly entertained in the highest rank of our public functionaries, what hope, it will be asked, can exist for an admission of the long unconsidered claims of the literary aspirant?

Thus unappreciated, neglected, despised, his enthusiasm and devotion weigh nothing against the patronage-sprung idler's rival pretensions, who, sot or fop, dunce or idiot, has credentials from—*"it matters not who!"* But, we ask, shall these things continue? shall this injustice never cease? shall our noblest workers be longer allowed to pine beneath the cold shade of social obscurity, while their great works are destined to enrich the stores of taste, wisdom, and erudition boasted by future ages? An answer, following swiftly as thunder succeeds to the near lightning, brands with indignant contempt the stolid indifference or insolent disdain betrayed in this official estimate of the right of learning and literary genius to a due recognition from the rulers of the State, in testimony of their high claims on public gratitude and national reward. While the name of a learned and ingenious writer shall be hailed as a glorious star in the firmament of the future, the memory of these degraded men in transient authority shall be but as the murky clouds that vainly sought to obscure its earlier beams, if indeed a total oblivion shall not have swept them from the record of the past. Should their images survive, they will assuredly be presented to the mind's eye of the future observer as mere subordinate figures introduced into the background of the picture, as adjuncts to the more prominent dignity of the main object, and subjected only to this degrading notice as the MIDAS-like deriders of immortal genius, or as the petty illiterate undervaluers of those stores of lofty erudition of which their humble, limited apprehensions could form no corresponding idea.

It is thus that Justice, sooner or later, strikes a balance between the deserving and the undeserving.

We will next consider what would be the effect of admitting our principal literary worthies to the higher official employments, of raising them to distinguished public honours, or of bestowing upon them an emolumentary provision, in acknowledgment of their great public services. Would it be for the advantage of the State, or otherwise? Would it be for the advantage of the men themselves, or otherwise?

First, then, as to the advantage of the State? The studies that refine and elevate the liberal mind must impart a sterling value to the labours of the literary worker. And those studies, therefore, should be encouraged and assisted by a provision for the exigencies of a writer's physical need, as regards personal support, and the maintenance of a fit social position, in order that he may be possessed of that due amount of leisure, and its attendant opportunities, which is calculated to enhance the value and success of his writings. A man labouring under depression of mind, beset with pressing pecuniary difficulties, deprived of necessary means of research, or of leisure to consider points of important interest in the process of literary speculations, must be expected to give birth to mental fruits of far inferior quality and quantity to those produced under more genial and kindly-fostering influences. Few, we believe, are the men now living, who, simply by the exercise of the pen, in the various departments of authorship, have raised themselves to an affluent position, or even maintained a condition free from degrading embarrassment. Our own experience of the habits and opinions of so-

ciety, as derived from a somewhat extended intercourse with persons of various classes, does
not favour the impression that literary men in
general hold that position in social life which
their superiority of mental accomplishments, and
widely - spread reputation, ought to command.
They are too frequently reckoned as amongst the
tribes of those "whom nobody knows." The
reason too often sufficing as an obvious explana-
tion of this most apparent ostracism of men of
literary merit from the upper circles of society,—
of this habitual estrangement of intercourse with
the more wealthy and influential portion of those
moving in a sphere of superior taste and refine-
ment, is the one understood and admitted fact,
that their worldly means are inadequate to the
demands inseparable from the attempt to maintain equal terms, or, in other words, support a
reputable position amongst people of ampler fortune. Were our lucrative civil employments conferred upon our more distinguished men of letters, they would be relieved from the necessity of
hiding those many talents and accomplishments
in unjust obscurity, which seem to have been imparted or acquired to give fascination and enjoyment to the social circle. It is too true that men
of the noblest intellect are pining in adversity,

whose works are well known to the reading
public, and from whose painful industry rich
publishers and prosperous booksellers are deriv-
ing copious profits. We may daily and hourly
see the antithesis presented by the author and
the mere trader upon his works. The former is
compelled to bury his days in the dull retirement
of some obscure suburb, too often the prey of
severe privation and anxious embarrassment;—
the latter pleasantly drives, when business is
over, in his handsome carriage, to some fashion-
able quarter near town, or takes the "express" for
Brighton, where his spacious mansion or elegant
villa, with all its attendant evidences of tasteful
opulence, evinces plainly enough the one-sided
bargains enforced upon the less fortunate, but far
more meritorious partner of his speculations. A
moderate pension, or appropriate official stipend,
would soon place deserved independence in the
path of the literary labourer. Minds like his
seek not to revel in voluptuous plenty, amid ob-
sequious friends and inordinate riches. His mental enjoyments would still possess for him the
highest charm in life. He would work with better
cheer, and with a prouder ambition to excel.
Add to this improvement of his means the prospect of a national mark of HONOUR as a prize for

conspicuous MERIT, and all has been done that can promise the means of sustaining emulation in the bosom of those who, with favouring opportunities, are born to give assured increase of honour to the literary annals of their country. In truth, society would reap, a hundredfold, the advantages of such an investment. We might then hope to see many proud additions to the stores of literary genius. Works that men would "not willingly let die," would soon replace the less elaborated compositions which a hurried necessity forces upon the public eye. Not then would our dramatic writers borrow openly and unscrupulously both the plots and dialogues of their pieces from the French stage. Our lyrical poets would restring their lyres, and invoke loftier influences to their aid. Our novelists would draw more steadily upon the higher resources of their taste and judgment, favoured by those anxiously-desired opportunities for leisurable criticism, so long and so imperiously forbidden to them. Marvellous results, now entirely unanticipated, would follow the royal proclamation that national honours and bounties would attend the display of conspicuous MERIT in every department of generous enterprise. Many a valuable manuscript, now buried in threatened insecurity, would be restored to the

eye of day, subjected to the severe revision of the
re-inspirited writer, amplified, enriched, and perfected with untiring skill and energy. The labours of science would be prosecuted with fresh
devotion, with bolder aspirations. The painter
and the sculptor would aspire to recall the triumphs
of a PARRHASIUS and a ZEUXIS, of a PHIDIAS and a
PRAXITELES, of a TIMANTHES and a PROTOGENES.
A new era would be inaugurated. The true spirit
of the ancients would return to us. "What a
collection of pygmies," exclaims an acute critic,
"do we now seem, compared with the gigantic
statues of the ancients!" Why should the un-
favourable contrast continue? We have their
powers of mind and body; but we want their *one
colossal virtue, the true source of power,—a reverence for mental and moral excellence,*—a belief in
our being able to approach by far nearer degrees
to perfection,—a steady, determined, unshrinking
will to accomplish the higher objects of a just
ambition. Give larger opportunities, more assured results, and we will prophesy a glorious
harvest of public advantage. A new era, rivalling
in splendour any that has preceded us, would present an assemblage of great characters formed on
the models of a better age, the age of AUGUSTUS
or of PERICLES. Our own country is not without

high examples for imitation in the noble reign of
ELIZABETH, which Englishmen should ever revere
and strive to emulate. "Give me a *fulcrum*,"
exclaimed ARCHIMEDES, "and I will move the
earth." The *fulcrum* was needed, but unattain-
able. That now required is attainable. It is the
all-potential voice of the Sovereign, calmly and
majestically uttering the plain, undeniable fact,
that, *in this wealthy and liberal country, there is
no fit provision made for the encouragement and
reward of those whose services to the State are most
deserving of its highest consideration.* Let our
various contributors to the press once feel their
liberation from the petty tyranny of their publishers' dictation, let them once find themselves
able to despise those impediments which now restrain their efforts to attain a due position in
social life,—and we shall see a Titanic and irre-
sistible power in the hands of a class which has
hitherto been chained and spell-bound, gagged
and fettered by the iron circumstances of NECES-
SITY. Authors will then band together in more
prominent clubs, and in more extended *coteries*.
They will meet fraternally in a wider and more
genial sphere of fellowship, welcomed in the
highest circles of society. There is a secret principle which unites kindred geniuses, as well as

c

kindred souls. The elevating influences of virtue
and knowledge, the dignifying behests of reason,
will gradually weaken the irrational prejudices
and erroneous modes of thinking that have been
rendered potential only as associated with the
want of all opposition, and they will give way,
one by one, beneath the lofty challenge of a purer
code of civilization, a far more spiritual and refined philosophy, a far nobler general system of
practical morality. The secret of these wide
social changes will be disclosed in the great successful fact that intellectual worth will assert and
maintain its long-impeded superiority, its just influences in the government of society. Happy
the day that shall behold the frigid convention-
alities of artificial life, the crude, insipid ideas of
caste and exclusiveness, the wide-spread laxity of
moral sentiment, the too-frequent absence of vital
religion, the low standard of personal honour,
yield to the nobler precepts of a new oracle, whose
inspiring divinity is VIRTUE, garbed in the noble
vestments of truth, knowledge, and beneficence,
and whose shrine is devoted to the honour and
happiness of human nature, while the ministrants
of her rites "are they who teach men to be wise,
virtuous, and happy,—the heralds of heaven,—
the messengers of peace and goodwill towards

man. Their voice is the voice of virtue, and its echo is glory." The dispensations of God have only one source, the will of Omnipotent Benevolence. "He who carefully imitates GOD," says the saintly ORIGEN, "is GOD's best statue!" Our prayer and hope are fervently assured that a better state of things looms in the future, that we shall see many "statues" raised, ere long, in high places, to GOD's honour and man's happiness.

The promotion of men of literary talent to public situations of trust and honour, as just recognitions of the claims of MERIT, and their increased social influence as the direct and beneficial result to society, have been sufficiently evidenced. Let us now consider what such a change of circumstances would operate upon "the men themselves," in addition to the incidents which have been brought into notice in the former part of our inquiry as to the result of "public" benefit.

"There is this good in commendation," says a writer of the last century, "that it helps to confirm men in the practice of VIRTUE."

"The praise," says PLUTARCH, "bestowed upon great and exalted minds, only spurs on and arouses their emulation. Like a rapid torrent, the glory already acquired hurries them irresistibly on to everything that is grand and noble."

"Gloriâ invitantur præclara ingenia," is proudly observed by Cicero. "True honour," says he, "is the concurrent approbation of good men; such only being fit to give their praise, who are themselves praiseworthy." And again he exclaims, "Why should we dissemble what it is impossible to conceal? Why should we not rather be proud of confessing, that we all aspire at glory; that this inclination is strongest in the noblest minds?" How have we to regret the loss of Cicero's Treatise on Glory, written by a man who in all parts of his conduct displayed so ardent a love of renown!

The generality of men are more or less influenced by motives that have their root in a love of HONOUR. If the spur of the spirit be not keen enough to impel them personally to seek the conflict in which the prize of gallantry is won, they more or less cordially sympathize with those who, bound to them by the ties of domestic or social relations, have been crowned with deserved tokens of national HONOUR. From ocean to ocean,—wherever humanity exists, whether savage or civilized, bond or free,—all covet, many deserve, marks of public distinction, as testimonies of their countries' approbation and gratitude,—those *priceless heirlooms* to be handed down, in memory of their achievements, to the latest posterity.

Glory—not wealth—is the aim of the intellectual labourer, as it is of all, indeed, who prefer a generous devotion of their lives and energies to the public service, rather than a mean care for the petty interests of selfish greed, or the baser allurements of vicious pleasure. Ere we proceed to point out the effects of royal and national favour on the fate of our literary contemporaries, let us make a few observations on the present sad lot of such worthies in this great and generous country.

Adverting to the well-known poverty and privations of this honourable class of men, well may parents exclaim with grateful emotion, " Oh, thank God, my son was not born a genius!" meaning one that was destined to become a lover of poetry and general literature, with a strong inclination for relinquishing the service of MERCURY to pay court to the MUSES. If some poor ill-fated wretch is discovered to be addicted to a passion for books and for literary composition, —if he is seen to eschew the common occupations and converse of the more ordinary people, and seek the congenial intercourse of a higher sphere of intellectual fellowship,—how soon do his wealthier kindred, even his more familiar associates, fall away from his side, not, perhaps,

without long and reiterated warnings of the
penalties to be paid for renouncing the comforts
and respectabilities of life, to engage in a course
of empty speculation which must too surely conduct him to misery and contempt.   Then, as
entreaties and remonstrances fail, they will resort
to the stronger hint of the "alienation from his
family," that must follow this mad decision.
" He will lose every friend he has on the earth !"
So ring out, in dolesome chimes, the *quasi-*
funereal chorus.   A later stage of expostulation,
in some instances, succeeds.   He is derided and
sneered at by some of these cork-headed, world-
incrusted wretches; his " visionary pretensions "
are exposed to the ready laugh, that bitter,
mocking expression of a coarse, malevolent nature !   Men must be superior to the world, while
they respect it, or be its slaves.   If, daring to be
WHAT HE IS (*ever a right maxim*), he persists in
following out what he conceives to be the appointed course of his destiny, namely, the aban-
donment of common pursuits to engage in a
career whose toils are virtue, and their reward,
honour; his relations and friends become, one by
one, estranged and cold, slowly, it may be, but
surely, dropping any connection or correspondence, leaving him, as they believe—and, it may

be suspected, hope—to his early and complete ruin. And well enough would it be, if the curtain were allowed to fall upon this stage of the plot. But there is too generally another and final act to be exhibited. Many a sad and sorrowful heart has found but too true the words of Shakespeare:—" Those you make friends and give your heart to, when they perceive the least rub in your fortunes, fall away like water from you, never found again unless they mean to *sink* you." These *worthy* relatives and friends must justify to the world their opinions, and the measures founded upon them. They are usually people, it must be understood, who stand much upon the " *respect* and *confidence* of *society*," the " *approbation* of *prudent* persons," *like* THEMSELVES! *Prudent!* it is a useful word in the mouth of clever worldlings. It so easily does duty for generosity, and for other qualities which are too apt to compel a reluctant fumbling for the purse that retreats into an angle of the pocket, as instinct with its owner's characteristic wariness, and cold, unsympathizing nature.

" In persons of this stamp," to quote a fine passage in a contemporary author, " dulness is caution; cowardice, discretion; and insensibility, virtue. Cold characters are the least likely to fall under censure; not having stimulus to move out of the beaten track, they remain behind a screen all their lives, alike inaccessible to the praise of the just, or the animadversions of the unjust. It is the ardent character who throws himself, body and soul, in the way of circumstances which demand opposition, that is the object of acclamation or opprobrium."

To proceed. The poor object of the aversion of these "*honourable* men," is now secretly maligned in every quarter, enemies are made for him in every direction. All communication ceases. A dark, ever-increasing shadow spreads itself over his future way. Nevertheless, his heart is brave—his soul is the home of conscious virtue—and he goes forth alone into the world, without a smile of sympathy from those whom PROVIDENCE seemed to have pointed out as his natural friends and allies. He goes forth, and it may be to perish.

We believe, that if we could ascertain the circumstances attending the earlier career, that is to say, the outset of almost every literary aspirant born in an honourable or respectable class of society, but unendowed with a competent share of this world's goods, we should find, more or less prominently exhibited, this emphatic denun-

ciation of his " misguided folly," this *brand* of a
" black sheep," sought to be affixed to his character, as an excuse and warrant for the sordid
abuse and base desertion of his miserable detractors, a desertion which simply and unmistakably
means, " Look not unto *us* in the day of evil.
On *your own* head let the consequences fall. Be
MAD—be MISERABLE." Thus they get rid of the
society of one, who, by adopting a precarious
and generally unremunerative pursuit, is likely
to fall into a chronic state of poverty and embarrassment.

If, as sometimes happens, the expected victim
gives promise to the public of high literary
ability, if the world begins to whisper of his
present success and future distinction,—a bastard
sort of envy, born of rooted contempt and com-
pulsory admiration, adds venom to the malignity
of his traducers. A curse sticks in their throat,
whenever his praise is casually resounded by the
organs of the press, or by those of human speech.
The selfish and the sordid are ever the most indefatigable calumniators, the fragrance of their
social respectability drowning the stink of their
moral infamy. But, alas for the destiny of our
gallant adventurer! " FORTUNE," as the elder
D'ISRAELI observes, " has rarely condescended to

be the companion of MERIT. Even in these en-
lightened times, men of letters have lived in
obscurity, while their reputation was widely
spread; and have perished in poverty, while
their works were enriching the booksellers."
" To mention those," he adds, " who left nothing
behind them to satisfy the undertaker, were an
endless task."

Few, we fear, are the instances in which the
hapless bark of the literary mariner is not seen
to go down in the stormy sea of worldly calamity.
Amongst a *hundred* strugglers for eminence in
authorship, does *one* (we ask the question with a
commiscrative sigh) does one succeed in securing
a reputable standing? Does more, indeed, than
one in a *thousand* reach the anticipated goal of
his ambition? The career of such a man is
often—

> " Too like the lightning, which doth cease to be,
> Ere one can say—it lightens!"

He fails, it is true; but, ere the heart-strings
break, or the brain is shattered, or the over-
whelming tempest of ghastly ruin sweeps him
away, he has probably given birth to some enduring assurance that he has not, like OCNUS in
classic writ, toiled in vain. He may have immortalized his name—that name so despised,

loathed, calumniated, and abjured by the *social respectabilities* of a former day; some great mental achievement may have entitled him to say, "Exegi monumentum ære perennius!" Dying in premature exhaustion and distress, he may yet smile on his fate, ascribing to the GOD who chose to model his nature and pursuits for His own concealed purposes, and to call His labourer from the work at the moment of His sovereign pleasure, the praise of the little which he has been permitted to accomplish, and feeling richly recompensed by the contemplation of any portion of benefit which his ungrateful contemporaries may have received, or which may be imparted to future generations.

GOD does not create men of this stamp in vain. They serve to manifest the more potential display of His revealed contempt for the ordinary teachings of the world. We ought not to look at such men as the slaves of misery—as outcasts beyond the social pale,—but rather, as those set apart, by a tangible mark, as the favourites of heaven, a mark which no ignorance can avoid seeing. Is it not too sad, that while we cannot but recognize this solemn ordination of their faculties to a superior mission in the cause of humanity,—while we see them direct every energy

of mind and frame to the one great object of
their thus consecrated lives,—we should yet, with
cold indifference, permit them to fall an almost
certain sacrifice to their sublime devotion ?

"But," to cite the eloquent words of KNOX,
"there was an inward satisfaction in conscious
rectitude, a generous spirit in heroic virtue,
which bore them through everything with comfort, and their merit increased and triumphed in
adversity."

The preceding picture, drawn from real life,
may be doubted by many worthy inexperienced
readers, who only think of an author of repute
as revelling in the pride of superior talents,
reading with complacency the praises of his
works in the magazines and newspapers, caressed
by noble and distinguished associates, the dar-
ling guest of the drawing-room and aristocratic
beauty, surrounded with the blessings conferred
by an elegant competency, and enjoying the
enviable charms of long intervals of enthusiastic
self-communion. Time was, when we ourselves
painted, for our heart's enjoyment, so blissful a
scene of imaginary happiness, but the cold reali-
ties of life have long ago banished the illusory
representation.

We think that enough has been said to evince

the present condition of men of learning and genius, and to show that indigence is the almost certain companion of literary merit. Let us pause for a moment, and consider why those men whom God Himself seems to honour most, should be least favourably regarded by their fellow-creatures. "On some He pours His spirit, on others He descends in showers of gold; and the moral to be drawn is this, that as He divides His benefits, so should men impart to each other a share of the gifts they have received from His goodness."

We have long wondered how it was possible that princes and nobles, and men of wealth and intelligence, professing honourable and liberal sentiments, could read the productions of a writer of genius, acknowledge the perfections of his style, the varied graces and beauties of his compositions, enrich their libraries with his valued tomes, expend their commendations upon the highly-gifted author,—yet, when the voice of public rumour disclosed the evidence of that author's embarrassments or ruin, could take no heed of the matter, even though to relieve that suffering would have cost but the lifting up of a finger—the utterance of a single word! How can it be, that neither individuals, nor the public

at large, feel any shame, or see any wrong, in
thus abandoning to his unhappy fate the noble-
minded supporter of his country's literary reputation amongst the kindred nations of the
globe? Of all human problems presented to us,
that of systematically ignoring the claims of eminent literary men struggling with the difficulties
of undeserved poverty, has ever been the most
difficult of solution—the most extraordinary and
unaccountable. We suppose, however, that the
sorrows of such sufferers are pondered upon for
a few transient moments, and forgotten. They
concern nobody individually; they moreover
suggest unpleasant ideas; the human mind na-
turally turns away from distress which it cannot
relieve; and the same feeling is entertained when
the past reveals its history of human sorrows.
But it is for the rulers of nations—for those who
have power to give force to the expression of
sentiment—it is for them, most unquestionably,
to guard the national honour of their respective
countries from the shameful reproach, that men
whose works do honour to their race, whose lives
are freely devoted to the good of mankind, in-
stead of being confined to the petty cares of self-
interest, should be permitted to exist in personal
obscurity and privation, and die in accordant dis-

tress and social contempt. The most speedy and
efficacious means of raising them to a just estimation in the eyes of the people, ought to be the
object of such rulers' special regard.

What a glorious world would this be, if things
were managed properly—not left to the "hurry-
skurry" of chance—not governed by the caprice
of passion or fancy—not exposed to the sinister
intrigues of concealed baseness,—but calmly, de-
liberately, wisely, and truthfully! There was an
ancient goddess to whom divine honours were
paid because she was supposed to grant success
and favour to good and useful intentions. Were
she now in possession of her former temple, we
would earnestly invoke her aid, while boldly, in
the face of unreflecting prejudice, or of that ab-
sorbing selfishness which is so often the ally of
wilful ignorance, we presume to argue that the
time is not distant when the cause we have so
feebly advocated in these pages will meet with a
fair attention, and the long-suppressed light of
justice prevail. The highest duties of our social
and political life are involved in a question which
has too long been neglected. That question can
only be fully apprehended, and rendered subser-
vient to the advancement of human happiness,
when an increased development of the true spirit

of civilization shall have prepared men's minds
for the adoption of juster views, and more equi-
table considerations. And that time, we trust,
is rapidly approaching, if it have not already ar-
rived. We think, indeed, it but requires a spark
of genuine patriotism, rightly directed, to ignite
a magazine of national enthusiasm, whose conta-
gious fervour shall quickly overpower the cold,
disdainful opposition of those short-sighted, class-
wedded politicians who are interested in perpe-
tuating the injustice of the past. Whether that
spark may be destined to proceed from the argu-
ments displayed in the present humble state-
ment, or be awakened by the appeal of a more
able and fortunate writer, we truly care not, and
shall be equally gratified to contemplate the success of the enterprise, whether it be due to our
own exertion, or to that of another, having no
literary reputation to seek, or individual interest
to sustain, in the furtherance of the object in view.
Our zeal is devoted to so good and honourable a
work for its own sake. To labour in such a cause
is to honour ourselves. That cause is the vindica-
tion of a high principle of national honour. The
question involved is that of the exclusion of our
most deserving "*public servants*" from the possession of "*public honours.*"

We would see, then, very gladly—and the sight would refresh every worthy heart in the realm—public rewards, both honorary and pecuniary, conferred on talents and virtues which are now—so far as State favour or royal appreciation can be supposed to be cognizant of them—buried in the depths of Cimmerian obscurity—veiled in Lethean oblivion—sunk in the impenetrable abysses of ancient Chaos. We would see appropriate pensions assigned not only to the learned historian, the erudite philologist, the accomplished linguist, the profound natural-philosopher, the refined poet, but also to the professors or representatives of the kindred arts—to the skilful painter, the expert engraver, the talented sculptor, the able musician, the ingenious mechanist, the deserving discoverer or inventor, or, in brief, to the whole united body of eminent civilians who have most conspicuously devoted their gifts and energies to the welfare and enjoyment of their fellow-men.

And, in order to distinguish more effectually those members of the commonwealth who have lived for the noble ends for which life was given, —who have spent their days in glorious toil, devoting their efforts to the highest aims of human ambition—to pursuits in which mediocrity is

D

failure, and in which only consummate excellence can claim the palm of success, for such men—*the noblest ornaments of their country*—we would boldly claim the grant of some mark of distinguished HONOUR at the hands of our national rulers.

We have a confident hope, that, old as we now are, we shall yet see the day when "this England of ours," not too proud to take a copy of the fine example set by every other European nation, shall choose to see the *equity*, and more than that—yes, far more than that in the estimation of our modern legislators,—the POLICY, of permitting the rills that derive their source from the "FOUNTAIN OF HONOUR" to extend themselves, albeit in tinier channels, to the distant region so long cut off from the fertilizing influence of that benignant irrigation.

The grant of a national symbol of MERIT would evoke marvellous results now entirely unanticipated. So coveted a boon would constitute a new motive power, the extent of whose force may be guessed, rather than approximately estimated. The establishment of the "LEGION OF HONOUR" in France, opened a new era in the national annals—it awoke a passionate sense of military glory, which the discerning founder knew well how to turn to account. He relied upon its influence, and it never failed him. In like manner, but as awakening the energies of our countrymen in the path of CIVIL MERIT, would an Order, in some respects similar to that of the " LEGION OF HONOUR," operate on the sensibilities of a British public.

We have long harped upon the national advantage of coining a new incentive to CIVIL VIRTUE—a recompense and source of encouragement for LITERARY, SCIENTIFIC, AND ARTISTIC MERIT. As far back as 1842, we wrote upon the subject with an anxious zeal. We repeated our efforts in 1848, and again, on two occasions, in 1855. And, in the intervals of those dates, we never ceased, through private correspondence, to urge eminent men of all departments of generous enterprise, to adopt this ardent view of ours, and seek to give vitality to its object.

Why? Because we saw in it the germ of boundless good for the advancement of our country's " dignity and honour," and for the promotion of the just happiness and welfare of thousands of yet unborn British subjects.

Proud will be the day that shall see created a National ORDER OF MERIT, accompanied in a limited number of instances, by a grant of

properly adjusted pensions, and enrolling in its
honoured ranks all whose services have given
them a valid claim to so enviable a distinction.
In most foreign orders exists the honourable
privilege of access to the Court. Let this be also
accorded as an incident to our English CROSS OF
MERIT. Let mental greatness, like the household
" clothed in scarlet" spoken of by SOLOMON,
" stand before princes." Why should not the
larger stars or planets approach nearest to the
sun? " The most things in this world," says an
old writer, " are perfectly imperfect; and the best
things but imperfectly perfect. This is assuredly
a very bad world when we have made the best of
it." Yet is this no reason why we should not
try to amend it. Every little step in the right
direction necessarily leads to good; and so surely
do steps in an opposite course conduct to evil.
From generation to generation, from year to
year, from day to day, by little and little, slowly
and slowly, are approaches made to a larger sum
of human happiness, wherever honest workers
are to be found—men asking no self-gain, giving
to GOD alone the glory for that which, through
His support, they may achieve, and richly rewarded if they see accomplished the noble ends
they have diligently sought to establish. Shall

the writer of this humble attempt to effect a high national advantage stay his pen from any portion of the task inviting his aid or influence, because he himself may not be personally interested in its success; because the undertaking affects in no perceptible manner his own private benefit? Shall the reader restrain his voice in support of it for the same reason? We will tell him that his children or later posterity may reap where he sows—reap with the gratitude due to his generous exertions. Every sentiment of humanity, of honour, of patriotism, and of religion itself forbids the selfish inquiry " What have I to do with this matter?" We answer with true Chilonian brevity (the people of Laconia never emphasized their words with greater terseness)—

" Reader, you are an Englishman."

We have treated of these matters in a spirit totally unprejudiced, and free from any interested calculation; biassed only by the sincerest love of our country, and influenced by an anxious regard for its " dignity and honour." To resume our argument. Titles ought to be marks set upon the highest worth. " Men of high MERIT (as suggested in our title-page) stamp a right to HONOUR with the seal of reflected eminence." Nobility without VIRTUE " is a fine setting without

a gem." Habits, titles, and dignities should not
be, as they too often are, "visible signs of invisi-
ble merits." We have, however, no objection to
the principle of establishing orders of ancestry, the
possession of which implies no high personal merit
in the members. Nobiliary distinctions, derived
from family descent and representation, indicate
no superiority beyond that of political and social
rank. We would as lieve think of stripping a
noble peer of his estates as of his *George* and
Garter, or other marks of royal favour. They
are becoming in the eyes of all loyal men, who
see in them the just incidents of a certain established position in the State. They often are the
due reward of political services, and in all cases
the meet adjuncts of high personal or hereditary
distinction. What we would see established is
the principle of perfect equality between man
and man in the sight of their common sovereign,
so far as refers to the right of competing on
equal terms as candidates for honorary recognition by the State; the possession of superior
VIRTUE (as defined in our first page) being the
principle that should determine the preference in
their favour. In such cases *birth* should give no
partial advantage. "HONOUR TO WHOM HONOUR IS
DUE" should ever be the ruler's cherished pre-
cept.

We should like to see the British monarch presiding at a "TRIBUNAL OF CONSCIENCE AND ORDERS," like that founded by the illustrious Emperor CHARLES THE FIFTH in Spain, forming a Council especially qualified to deal with the question of chivalric awards in all its complicated bearings—a solemn and authentic mode of administering the grant of public honours, which precluded, as far as human foresight could effect, the malversations of courtly and other intriguers for such ostensible marks of national gratitude. No mean artifices or shifts could betray the eye of that astute ruler; and, as the founder of that council, or "TRIBUNAL OF CONSCIENCE AND ORDERS," an institution of great national advantage worthy of imitation in other countries, we honour his imperial memory. Over this tribunal or council, call it what we may please, the Sovereign should sit as Supreme Director, assisted by its various officers and members. We have a "BOARD OF TRADE," a "BOARD OF GREEN CLOTH," and other "BOARDS;" why not then have a "BOARD OF CONSCIENCE AND ORDERS," or rather, let us say, a "COURT OF HONOUR"? Under its especial and peculiar jurisdiction should be brought all claims or petitions to chivalric and nobiliary distinctions without the mediation of "*It matters not who.*" No influen-

tial patron or supporter should have a voice in
the selection of honorary recipients. All pro-
ceedings should be free from the repression or
mistaken depreciation of any ministerial, official,
or courtly "go-between;" they should be di-
rectly, openly, nakedly conducted, in the eyes of
all men, in the light of perfect day.

The *insignia* of an ORDER OF MERIT would unmistakably speak of personal, not of positional or
adventitious eminence. There need then be no
jealousy between the possessors of these various
and dissimilar dignities. The influence of an
ORDER OF MERIT FOR CIVIL SERVICES on the views
and habits of general society would be electrical.
How men's ideas would change when they saw
royal and national honours showered in just pro-
fusion upon deserving men, whose patient and
modest acceptance of the rough conditions of this
sordid world had seemed to chain them to a
doom of chronic wretchedness, to a fate of almost
hopeless obscurity, their great talents, their
superhuman industry alike ignored or despised
by the mob of worthless worldlings that surrounded them !

Yes, the glorious beams of the royal luminary
should be as free and benignant as those of the
sun of nature, whose splendour is regulated by

the Divine Ruler. No petty screens should be set up to check or intercept its more lavish radiance. The " FOUNTAIN OF HONOUR " exists as a national source of blessing and blessedness. It is the sacred stream destined to impart verdure and luxuriance to the arid soil of fields of peril and of labour, wherever persevering courage and talent win the hardly earned palm of just distinction. Every native of our vast empire has a personal appeal to its appointed ministration as the distributive medium of the nation's rewards for distinguished VIRTUE as a citizen. The love of glory is the prevailing influence that stimulates men of all classes to deeds of lofty exertion. Take away the noble prize of HONOUR, and the best incentive to excel in arts or arms is lost.

The " FOUNTAIN OF HONOUR " is the most august and expressive image that can represent the regal office, save only its sister emblem, the " FOUNTAIN OF JUSTICE." The " FOUNTAIN OF HONOUR " exists as a national source of favour to reward the good. The " FOUNTAIN OF JUSTICE " has for its implied attribute the punishment of the evil. By a strictly logical necessity, both " FOUNTAINS " should find their waters directed in corresponding channels to the furthest boundaries of the wide area of the commonwealth.

The analogy is perfect; the inference unques-
tionable. "The good actions of men," says
SOLON, the wisest of all human legislators, "are
produced by the fear of punishment and the hope
of reward." There has been little hesitation or
difficulty in arranging a system of punishment.·
The stream from this "FOUNTAIN" has been
copiously administered, and its waters have too
often been blended *with a darker fluid*, while it
has been the labour of patriotic and humane
minds to seek to render more precious in the
eyes of those in power the lives of their erring
fellow-creatures. To dispense the genial lymph
that flows from the twin "FOUNTAIN," so that all
who eminently deserved might enjoy an invigo-
rating draught from its salubrious *reservoir*, has
been held a less practicable or desirable function
by those to whom were mainly delegated the
sovereign's privileges in regard to the exercise
of this, the loftiest right of the imperial CROWN.
But let us reverently recall the pleasing fact that
no complaint of neglect in respect of any alleged
invidious privation is to be referred to the personal indifference of the monarch who, in our own
day, combines every quality of heart and mind
most supremely conducive to the happiness of
her loving subjects. What the Romans said of

Titus, Englishmen may apply to their present Queen, for, whithersoever she goes, she is the "love and delight of all men."

Well do we all know the truthful axiom—"The King *reigns*, but the minister *rules*,"—an axiom that has repeated itself in the fellow-saying—"The King can do no wrong." There is good in this, and there is harm, as must generally occur in all human arrangements. "Every medal has its reverse." Every convenience carries its abatement. The harm alluded to, as connected with the good, is the diminution of paternal and filial reciprocity between the sovereign and the subject, as necessarily occasioned by this enforced delegation of personal authority. We still apply to our Kings the title of "SIRE" or "FATHER," and we have yet a sincere and strong meaning in the use of the epithet. The idea of favour softens and renders less invidious the more severe sentiment associated with that of power. We love to see the "FATHER" in the "KING," and to look upon him in the light of a chief "BENEFACTOR." The highest title of the Omnipotent Ruler, as expressed in the ascription of man's devoted gratitude, is that of "FATHER." In the days of pagan superstition, the most powerful of all the reputed gods received the name of JUPITER, *quasi* JUVANS

PATER. "EUERGETES," a surname signifying "BE-
NEFACTOR," was commonly given to many kings
in ancient times. And with what pleasure does
our eye rest on the names of those admirable men
who used power for the noblest end—*that of be-
friending* MERIT; while we turn aside with contempt and loathing from the record of those
baser souls that regarded it only as valuable for
the furtherance of their own selfish aims and
purposes! Who could have greater honour than
AGESILAUS, King of Sparta, who was fined by the
EPHORI for having stolen all the hearts of the
people to himself? of whom it is said, that he
ruled his country by *obeying* it? Beautiful is the
address of the Roman Senate to the second CLAU-
DIUS—"CLAUDI Auguste, tu frater, tu pater, tu
amicus, tu bonus senator, tu vere princeps."

To do good to his subjects was the ambition of
TITUS, and it was at the recollection that he had
done no service, or granted no favour one day,
that he exclaimed, "I have LOST a day!" There
spoke the soul of a prince—the spirit of a true
man—the "FATHER"—the "BENEFACTOR" of his
people.

We read with a sense of grateful pleasure that
VESPASIAN, the parent of this good Prince, was
equally conspicuous for his many virtues. To

men of learning and merit he was very liberal; one hundred thousand sesterces were annually paid from the public treasury to the different professors that were appointed to encourage and promote the arts and sciences. It was a fine compliment made to this excellent man—"Greatness and majesty have changed nothing in you but this, that your *power* to do good should be answerable to your *will.*"

It was Roman VIRTUE that raised the Roman glory. The greater a man is in power above others, the more he ought to excel them in VIRTUE; wherefore CYRUS said, "that none ought to govern who was not better than those he governed." There is no true glory, no true greatness, without VIRTUE.

Men of eminent note, as poets, philosophers, and scholars, were much regarded by monarchs in the ancient world. VIRGIL, HORACE, LIVY, CATULLUS, CORNELIUS NEPOS, PROPERTIUS, TIBULLUS, OVID, CRISPINUS PLOTIUS, VARIUS, and other literary men, were admitted to various degrees of intimacy by AUGUSTUS. AUGUSTUS was very affable, and returned the salutation of the meanest individual. One day a person presented him with a petition, but with so much awe that AUGUSTUS was displeased with his meanness. "What, friend!" cried he; "you seem as if you were offering something to an elephant, and not to a man; be bolder."

What says glorious old SHAKESPEARE, the oracle of human wisdom and moral truthfulness?

> " Mock not flesh and blood
> With solemn reverence—
> Abstain from semblance of servility ;
> And by thy body's action teach the mind
> A most inherent baseness."

It has been justly remarked by a writer of our own day, that " this maxim is drawn from the depths of human nature and moral philosophy, and expressed with the same sublimity as it was conceived." Genuflection and prostration are some of the slavish modes of paying civil respect throughout the barbarous East, unmeet for civilized usage. LOUIS XVI. of France, FREDERICK THE GREAT of Prussia, and JOSEPH, Emperor of Germany, all, it is said, forbade kneeling to them.

But to pursue our former train of remark. In the records of modern times we read of but few instances of a close sympathy between the *savant* and the sovereign. It is honourable to the memory of GEORGE THE FIRST, if true, that, being told by some one how happy he was to be King of England and Elector of Hanover at the same time, he said, " I am prouder of being able to say I have two such subjects as NEWTON and LEIBNITZ in my dominions, than to say I reign over the kingdoms that contain them." This anecdote reminds us of another, told of FRANCIS THE FIRST of France, who encouraged letters and the fine arts from a real love he had for them. When BENVENUTO CELLINI told him how happy he was to have the patronage of so great a Prince, FRANCIS replied most nobly, " I am as happy to have so great an artist as yourself to patronize." He gave great pensions to men of letters, particularly to BUDÆUS.

Recent cases of a personal attachment bordering on familiar friendship exist in the anecdotes preserved by VON HUMBOLDT and ANDERSEN in reference to their respective sovereigns, the late Kings of Prussia and Denmark. Another instance of princely regard towards the mentally great of his own and other countries may be cited in the person of the present Emperor of the French, himself a man of much literary taste and talent, whose frequent and favoured guests are selected from the ranks of learning and genius. Such intimacies convey unmistakably to such favoured individuals the precious assurance that their worth is widely acknowledged—that their

names will live in the estimation of mankind—an
assurance far more acceptable than the possession
of piles of gold, or heaps of bank-notes. Alas,
that such pleasing pictures of elevated sympathy
between minds of congenial character, as prevailing in opposition to the restraining effects of a
contrariety of worldly station, should be so rare
in these vaunted days of superior enlightenment,
when it might be thought that there would exist
a more general appreciation of the value and dignity of the services rendered to the community
by men of letters and scientific students, the far
greater number of whom are permitted to live
"in cold obscurity,"—poor and unknown! One
would think that the greatest honour of human
life was to live well with men of merit. We believe that the fact arises from this melancholy
truth, that few princes, like the French Emperor,
possess a refined taste of letters, which alone can
give a zest for the happy communication of just
and generous sentiments, the display of luxuriant
fancy, and of the variety of knowledge and other
triumphs of intellectual superiority. To souls
unanimated with noble views, nature and fortune
have only assigned material advantages to be
misapplied. In such souls a zeal for the public
good, and a pride in that merit which is its best

support, cannot live. The "imperial purple" may flow gracefully over the shoulders of the wearer, while the pomp that is born of nature in the mind, and attired in the ornaments of a diligent culture, exists not within the breast that glitters beneath the gorgeous star of a merely external and lifeless grandeur.

The generosity and favour of monarchs are beautifully illustrated in many of the most stirring passages of our earlier history. They present traits of royal life and princely bearing which are excluded, too generally, from the observation of modern experience. They are "parcel of the past," and, in such instances, the past returns no more. JUPITER himself, as classical fables tell us, was forced to submit to the decrees of the FATES. And so, in like manner, must modern potentates submit to the unavoidable causes which tend to sever a personal intercommunion with the bulk of even their most distinguished subjects. They must be chiefly seen when exercising the displays of courtly ceremonials—when acting their august part in the befitting pageantries of their royal station. The monarch of to-day must necessarily be unknown in person to millions of his most dutiful and devoted lieges. In earlier times, his face and form, his manners and speech, would

have been familiar to the meanest of his people.
In those days it was, as we have seen, that the
title of "FATHER" was addressed, as significant
of the ruler of a nation. With more or less sig-
nificancy has it been the wont of all peoples,
from the earliest records of the world, to call their
rulers by the same touching and expressive title.
Nations then consisted of mere families, patri-
archally governed, and the king was in most respects simply the first of his people, sharing as
an individual in all their common sympathies,
bred up in their own habits, affected, like themselves, by every circumstance of success or failure, enjoyment or suffering. Wide changes in
the constitution of human society have generated
corresponding alterations in social manners and
ideas; but still, from the force of early associa-
tions, as perpetuated by our mental pictures of
scenes exhibited in the life of the earlier ages, we
have clung to the use of the endearing term of
"SIRE" or "FATHER," as expressive of the love
which a sovereign bears to his people, and of that
which a people bear to their monarch as his implied *children*. Every act on the part of his appointed ministers that tends to disturb or dimi-
nish these ties of reciprocal affection and respect
should be scrupulously deprecated and avoided,

as dangerous to the foundations of the great social compact.

The high rewards for great national services are entrusted by the people to the hand of the reigning sovereign, who is advised as to their distribution by a "responsible" minister. The minister is "responsible," of course, to the people as well as to the CROWN—alike to the governing and the governed. It is the right of the sovereign to command, the duty of the subject to obey, both being alike directed in their actions by the obligation of constitutional laws. Sovereign and subject are alike accountable to a higher Power than that which human laws can frame; and to which Power most especially are "responsible" those to whom are committed the awful duties of rulers over mankind. What higher motive, then, can inspire a monarch to rule with unswerving justice and equity than the prevailing conviction of this inevitable accountability to the Supreme Throne?

To that just and awful sense of royal responsibility we reverently and most loyally and lovingly, as a dutiful and attached British subject, appeal for the removal of a flagrant obstruction to the cause of right—namely, the regulation, of long usage, which dispenses grants of honour, and

other distinctions and advantages, to those who
are recognised as "*servants of the State;*" while
the representatives of that far nobler and more
deserving class which has made England what
she is in the estimation of her sister nations, and
in the pride of her own heart, as the land of
SHAKESPEARE and MILTON, of BACON and NEWTON,
are shut out from the distribution of "*State rewards;*"—an injustice which is only imperfectly
repaired by the occasional munificence of the
rulers of other countries, who have, with the most
noble generosity, admitted British subjects, distinguished by *literature, science, and art,* into
their several ORDERS OF MERIT.

What do we mean when we talk of civilization,
when we speak contemptuously of the heathen
ages of the various races of our species? Do we
so often meet with a sordid neglect of men of
learning and genius in the days we thus asperse?
No; we read of most numerous instances in which
the highest honours, royalty included, were
heaped upon them. It were well, indeed, if we
tore a few leaves out of the nobler volume of the
past, and strove to profit by the bright example
they would give to us. In the history of ancient
times there only occur to our immediate recollection five instances wherein distinguished literary

talents brought no corresponding advantages to their possessors.

The list of unfortunate men of letters living in modern times abounds with incidents of the most revolting calamity and neglect, as we seek to show in the latter portion of our volume. Yet, large as is the list, it might have been far extended, had our leisure permitted; but the examples that we have given of the miseries they endured are sufficiently complete for the purpose in view.

We cannot close this brief appeal without a consoling glimpse at the less obvious facts that accompanied the sad experiences of these seemingly ill-fated worthies. Their lot was not all bitterness. The direst visitations of misfortune could not stifle the deep inward satisfaction which the noble enthusiast enjoyed in perfecting the immortal works of his pen. For a time he forgot the earth, and, like the prophet of old, "his soul was in heaven." If the sneer of the dull worldling derided his unselfish labours—if the cold, calculating pursuers of wealth sought to place on him a *stigma* that degraded him in the social *census*, prating, as our political economists prate, of the "recognised necessities and common fitness" of things, and freely assigning, as a "satisfactory result," a condition of deserved poverty with its attendant privations, to those who "chose to labour for others rather than for themselves," we smile at the thought which assures us that the retirement of the thus calumniated bard or philosophic student was a sacred retreat from the ungenial scenes of the world without—an asylum into which no unhallowed impeachment of his generous devotion and inspired toils could intrude, and in which he could uninterruptedly dream over his happy hopes of immortal honour, without the least thought of the sneer of his ignorant and vulgar-minded detractors. Those small-brained, heartless, wealth-esteeming, and stupid worldlings now sleep the inglorious sleep of the unheeded and worthless dead; forgotten—or despised, if remembered.

What says the high-souled Roman writer? "Mors omnibus ex natura æqualis est : oblivione apud posteros, vel gloria distinguitur."

The "glorious few" repose in revered quietude; their brief struggles with poverty and misfortune are but upbraiding memories for those who survive. Their noble works are labelled with the title of "immortal;" and their spirits are revelling in the boundless bliss of the mansions of heaven. They enjoy the rich "rewards"

perpetually and blessedly flowing from a " Fountain of Honour " whose dignities are eternal ;
and they bask in the blaze of the Great Throne
of Universal Dominion, whose Omnipotent Lord
is, was, and ever will be, through interminable
and nightless *ages* (so to speak of eternity, which
is ever *new*) the true " Father " and " Benefactor " of all His peoples.

Glean we, by way of illustration, a few prominent examples of the various fortunes experienced by men of genius and learning in ancient and modern times.

So great was the veneration of the people of Magna Græcia for the celebrated philosopher PYTHAGORAS, that he received the same honours as were paid to the immortal gods, and his house became a sacred temple.

EMPEDOCLES, the philosopher, poet, and historian, of Agrigentum, was offered the crown of his country, which he refused.

The Athenians were so pleased with the "*Antigone*" of SOPHOCLES, at the first representation, that they presented the author with the government of Samos.

PLATO was bidden by the second Dionysius to appear at his court, and accepted the invitation. So far, philosophy was honoured in his person; but not all his eloquence could prevail upon that cruel tyrant to become the father of his people. The works of this great writer, who justly received the epithet of "divine," were so famed for the elegance, melody, and sweetness of expression, that their author became distinguished by the appellation of the "Athenian Bee." His opinions were universally received and adopted.

The people of Stagira instituted public festivals in honour of the memory of the famous ARISTOTLE, of whom it has been said that he has exercised as wide a dominion over men's minds as his famous pupil Alexander did over nations. It has been said of ARISTOTLE that he was the "Secretary of Nature;" he "dipped his pen in intellect."

To establish public holidays—days of general recreation and enjoyment—in memory of a great benefactor, seems the most judiciously-considered reward that could be decreed to departed worth.

Kings and princes were desirous of the friendship of THEOPHRASTUS, the successor of Aristotle in the Lyceum. Cassander and Ptolemy regarded him with uncommon tenderness.

When Alexander passed through Phaselis, he crowned with garlands the statue which had been erected to the memory of the Greek orator and poet, THEODECTES.

The Bœotian poet and musician, TIMOTHEUS, was a great favourite of Alexander. Another and earlier poet and musician of the same name, of Miletus, received an immense sum of money from the Ephesians, in recompense of a poem which he had composed in honour of Diana.

XENOCRATES, the Platonic philosopher, was courted, though with no success on their part, by Philip of Macedon and his son Alexander. Though respected and admired, he was poor; and he was dragged to prison because he was unable to pay a small tribute to the State. He was soon delivered from his confinement by one of his friends.

EUCLID was the preceptor and friend of Ptolemy Philadelphus.

THEOCRITUS, the Greek poet, enjoyed the favours of the same prince.

Scipio desired to be buried by the side of his poetical friend ENNIUS. Could a higher honour be accorded to human merit?

CATULLUS directed his satire against Cæsar, whose only revenge was to invite the poet to a good supper. We Christian pietists may occasionally take a hint from lessons afforded by the history of heathen times.

SALLUST, the Latin historian, was made quæstor

and consul, and afterwards became Governor of Numidia, through the favour of Cæsar.

PUBLIUS SYRUS, a Syrian mimic poet, originally a slave sold to Domitius, gained the esteem of the most powerful at Rome, and reckoned Julius Cæsar among his patrons.

VIRGIL, OVID, HORACE, PROPERTIUS, TIBULLUS, CORNELIUS NEPOS, and a host of other illustrious writers, were the favoured friends of Augustus.

VIRGIL received from Augustus 10,000 sesterces for every verse in the "*Æneid*" referring to Marcellus, while Octavia, the emperor's sister, mother of the deceased youth, the subject of his panegyric, liberally rewarded him.

The "*Æneid*," remarks Huet, Bishop of Avranches, one of the most illustrious scholars of modern times, "was declared a work which conferred on VIRGIL the title of the most illustrious of all Roman writers. Those who dared to depreciate this excellent poem were held as profane and impious persons. The Roman people, in a crowded theatre, on hearing some verses recited from their favourite author, rose from their seats, to show their veneration for the poet, and, on hearing that he was then in the theatre, they showed the same marks of respect with which they would have received Augustus himself."

The great abilities of TIMAGENES, a Greek historian of Alexandria, gained the favour of Augustus.

CICERO was styled the "Father of his Country, and a second Founder of Rome." What higher titles could he enjoy? His chequered career is so well known as to need no other comment.

ROSCIUS, the celebrated Roman actor, may be mentioned in the present series of men of genius, as the author of a treatise in which he compared, with much judgment and learning, the profession of the orator with that of the comedian. In his private character he was so respectable that he was raised to the rank of senator. His daily stipend for acting was a thousand *denarii*, or about £32. 6s. English money; though Cicero makes his yearly income to be about £48,334.

A son of ZENO, the rhetorician, was made King of Pontus by Antony.

What will our modern physicians think of the rewards conferred by Augustus on his physician, ANTONIUS MUSA, who cured his master of a dangerous disease by recommending him the use of the cold bath? He was honoured with a brazen statue by the Roman Senate, which was placed near that of Æsculapius, and Augustus permitted him to wear a golden ring, and to be exempted from all taxes.

LUCAN, the poet and historian, was raised by Nero to the dignity of an augur and quæstor before he had attained the proper age.

SULPITIUS, the orator, was employed as an ambassador, and, at his death, the Senate and the Roman people, at the instigation of Cicero, erected a statue to his honour in the Campus Martius.

PETRONIUS, an author of exceptionable morals, but possessed of a pen of extreme elegance, was appointed proconsul of Bithynia, and afterwards consul; in both of which employments he behaved with all the dignity becoming the successors of a Brutus or a Scipio.

The historian TACITUS was honoured with the consulship.

The elder PLINY was courted and admired by the emperors Vespasian and Titus, but it is doubtful whether his literary works alone were considered as a reason for this distinction. He was born of a noble family, and had held several high public offices, in which his prudence and abilities made him respected. He employed his days in the administration of the affairs of his province, and the nights were devoted to study.

MARTIAL, the famous epigrammatist, received the highest honours from Domitian, who, amongst other distinctions, raised him to the tribuneship.

SUETONIUS, the Latin historian, was treated with peculiar favour by the emperor Adrian.

PLINY *the younger* presided over Pontus and Bithynia in the office of proconsul.

The emperor Trajan admired the abilities of PLUTARCH, honoured him with the office of consul, and appointed him governor of Illyricum. He had opened a school in Rome, which was much frequented. His *"Lives of Illustrious Men"* will be read as long as admiration for virtue shall live in the hearts of men.

POLEMON, a sophist, of Laodicea, was greatly favoured by Adrian.

EPICTETUS, the Stoic philosopher, enjoyed the esteem and friendship of the emperors Adrian and Marcus Aurelius. But he preferred poverty to riches, and resided in a cottage which had no furniture but an earthen lamp, which was sold after his death for 3000 drachmas.

The emperor Marcus Aurelius was so sensible of the merit of LUCIAN, the author of the *"Dialogues"* and other admirable compositions, that he made him registrar to the Roman governor of Egypt, a post of high emolument and dignity.

The Roman emperor Caracalla was so pleased with the poetry of OPPIAN that he gave him a piece of gold for every verse of his poem entitled *"Cynegeticon,"* from which circumstance the poem received the name of the "golden verses" of OPPIAN.

PLOTINUS, a Platonic philosopher, became a public teacher in Rome, and was caressed by Gallienus, who admired the extent of his learning. His eloquence charmed the populace, his doctrines the senate; his school was frequented by people of every sex, age, and quality, and he was a universal favourite.

LONGINUS, the philosopher and critic, of Athens, became minister to Zenobia, the famous Queen of Palmyra. He was one of her favourites, and taught her the Greek tongue. Admired for her literary, as well as military talents, she received no less honour from the patronage she afforde to that celebrated critic.

AURELIUS VICTOR, a writer in the age of Constantius, was greatly esteemed by the emperor, and honoured with the consulship.

LIBANIUS, the celebrated sophist, of Antioch, contemptuously refused the offers of the Emperor Julian, who wished to purchase his friendship and intimacy by raising him to offices of the greatest splendour and affluence in the empire.

THEMISTIUS, the philosopher, was high in the esteem of the Roman emperors, and raised to the senate.

Only five instances immediately occur to our recollection in which distinguished literary merit brought no corresponding advantages to the possessor. They are those of Homer, Socrates, Cleanthes, Plautus, and Xylander.

HOMER, justly esteemed, in succeeding ages, the "Prince of Poets," possessing power over the human heart which might almost be called magical, lived as a homeless wanderer, resorting to public places to recite his verses for a morsel of bread,—glad to receive from the hand of the coarsest clown the meanest dole. If the story of Belisarius be, as is supposed by the generality of our ablest scholars, a fiction of modern invention, the hideous fact of Homer's mendicancy is without a parallel in the records of public infamy. Some authors doubt the truth of the story as to HOMER's blindness, and equally dispute the question of his poverty. "*Nox alta velat*."

XENOPHANES, a Greek philosopher of Colophon, author of many poems and treatises, and founder of the Eleatic sect in Sicily, died very poor when about 100 years old.

A life of poverty, labour, and hardship was led, by choice, by that greatest of all moral philosophers, the illustrious SOCRATES. Insults, injuries, and contempt were showered upon him. He was ridiculed and hated for his superiority of mind and independence of spirit, and at length exposed, by public injustice, to death by poison. All succeeding ages have venerated his exemplary virtue. He died at the summit of mortal glory.

CLEANTHES, the "Father of the Stoics," as Cicero calls him, was so poor that to maintain himself he used to draw out water for a gardener in the night, and study in the daytime. Yet this great man was the successor of Zeno. He ended his noble yet wretched life in characteristic suffering. It is said that he starved himself in his 90th year.

The excellent comic poet PLAUTUS, in order to maintain himself, entered, it is said, into the family of a baker, as a common servant. Varro, whose judgment is great, declares that if the Muses were willing to speak Latin, they would speak in the language of PLAUTUS. His comedies, twenty-five in number, were written at spare moments snatched from his daily toil.

One poor solitary dinner was the sole recompense obtained by a starving writer of note, XYLANDER, for his laboriously compiled "*Annotations on Dion Cassius.*"

Let us now descend to modern times, and see what they will present to us.

F

DANTE's fate has met with the following beautiful but melancholy record from a pen of our own day :—

> " His, alas ! to lead
> A life of trouble, and ere long to leave
> All things most dear to him, ere long to know
> *How salt another's bread is, and the toil*
> *Of going up and down another's stairs.*"

THEODORE GAZA, an eloquent writer both in the Greek and Latin languages, a distinguished reviver of ancient learning, was equally unfortunate, and "adds to the number of those whom Providence has exhibited to prove that the rewards of virtuous and useful labour do not consist in riches, honours, or anything else which the rulers of this world are able to bestow." Poor GAZA had dedicated his " *Translation and Commentaries on Aristotle's Book on Animals* " to Pope Sixtus the Fourth, in hopes of procuring from his patronage a little provision for his old age. The Pope gave him only a purse with a few pieces in it, and accompanied his gift with a manner which induced GAZA to conclude that it was the last favour he should receive. GAZA received it in silence ; and as he walked home, all melancholy and indignant, along the banks of the Tiber, he threw the purse into the stream, and soon after died of vexation and disappointment.

PHILELPHUS, whose writings partake much of the graces which shine so agreeably in the epistles of Pliny and Cicero, after a long life of laborious application, during which he was honoured by the friendship of princes and Pontiffs, died, in his eighty-second year, so poor that his bed and the utensils of his kitchen were sold to pay the expenses of his funeral.

The truly venerable ALDUS MANUTIUS was so lamentably destitute of means, that the cost incurred in the removal of his library from Venice to Rome reduced him to the state of an insolvent.

The squalid walls of a workhouse surrounded the death-bed of the renowned AGRIPPA.

ERASMUS was certainly the greatest man of his time. Popes, kings, archbishops, bishops, and cardinals hid their diminished heads in his presence. One is, indeed, almost tempted to laugh when one surveys a group of stupid personages with crowns and mitres, riches and titles, sitting on their thrones and in their cathedrals, yet bowing with an homage at once abject and involuntary, to the personal merit of the poor, neglected, unpreferred ERASMUS. He was permitted by Providence to perform a pilgrimage through this world without ecclesiastical riches or dignity; he was designed as an instance to prove that great merit is its own reward, and that temporal distinctions are allowed, like trifles beneath the notice of Heaven, to fall indiscriminately on the deserving and the undeserving, the learned and the ignorant. ERASMUS had no mitre; but he had the internal satisfactions of genius; he had glory, he had liberty, and the wearers of mitres crouched at the awful dignity of his personal merit.*

LOUIS CAMOENS, the greatest literary genius ever produced by Portugal, died, in his native city of Lisbon, in the greatest destitution. How touching is the fact, that while his country beheld his wants with ingratitude and neglect, he was chiefly maintained by the unwearied efforts of an old black servant, who had been long the faithful companion of his distresses. This devoted follower, a native of the island of Java, begged alms in the streets of Lisbon; and the scanty pittance thus casually acquired was the sole support of his dying master. Yet has no record that we have ever seen perpetuated the name of this noble and exalted Indian ! Were we privileged to exercise the astronomer's choice, in giving to a newly-discovered planet a designation by which it should be known through all future ages, we

* Knox's ' Essays,' vol. iii. p. 63, 17th edit.

would seek to ascertain the name of this faithful attendant, and rejoice in the opportunity of transmitting it thus conspicuously, as that of the recorded luminary. But his name already shines in heaven with a brighter glory than that of star or planet—where the highest boast of earthly distinction is but as—

> " A tale
> Told by an idiot, full of sound and fury,
> Signifying nothing!"

Tasso claims the following melancholy notice from the pen of one of our most esteemed modern poets :—

> " His to drink deep of sorrow, and through life,
> To be the scorn of them that knew him not,
> Trampling alike the giver and his gift,
> The gift a pearl precious, inestimable,
> A lay divine, a lay of love and war,
> To charm, ennoble, when the oar was plied,
> Or on the Adrian or the Tuscan sea."

Tasso, while enjoying the laudatory title of " the Great," half playfully, half earnestly alludes to his occasional privations, in one of his sonnets addressed to a favourite cat, entreating her to bestow, during the darkness of the night, the lustre of her eyes, " non avendo candele per iscrivere i suoi versi ! " To borrow from one of his friendly admirers so small a sum as a crown to meet the demand for ordinary necessaries seems to have been no infrequent act. Had he or the nation the deeper cause to blush for his exposure to such an indignity?

LYDIAT, an eminent writer, was not less famous for his learning than his misfortunes, and was respected by the scholars of his age, while some foreign *literati* ranked him with Lord Bacon.

The younger SCALIGER, who has been called " The Abyss of Erudition" and " The Ocean of Science," deplored all his lifetime the want of patronage, and the straitness of his circumstances.

The learned English monarch, James the First, took great pleasure in reading, night after night, the valuable work of PURCHAS—the ' *Relation of the World,*' which the author had spent years of distant travel and unremitting toil in preparing for the press. The King read it, we are told, " with great profit and satisfaction," but allowed the meritorious writer to be thrown into prison at the suit of the printer, as the reward of his long and anxious labours. This able and indefatigable writer died in the most indigent circumstances.

With all his incomparable merit, with all the

celebrity of his name, MICHAEL CERVANTES, immortalized by his admirable satire of '*Don Quixote*,' had to maintain a miserable fight with the coarsest necessities of an obscure station. He had at times difficulty to preserve himself from the horrible fear of starvation. Some writers, indeed, record that he perished in the streets from hunger.

JOHN KEPLER, one of the greatest philosophers that ever lived, and whom some regard as the discoverer of the true system of the world, died in poverty. Thus did this eminently great and good man leave nothing to his wife and children but the remembrance of his talents and virtues.

Anthony Wood informs us that OWEN, the celebrated Latin epigrammatist, was much distressed by poverty, the "epidemical disease of poets."

It is perhaps allowable for us to believe that SHAKESPEARE, with all his wonderful powers as a writer, would have barely earned a livelihood as an author. The munificence of his patron, Lord Southampton, and his prosperous speculations as a theatrical manager, too probably were the only circumstances that absolved society from the bitter shame it would have incurred, if a genius like his had dragged down its possessor to the desti-

tution too generally the reward of great talents
employed in authorship.

EDMUND SPENSER is said to have died of hunger
in the streets of Dublin. Let us now see how "rare
BEN JONSON" fared amongst his contemporaries.

A LETTER TO THE EARL OF NEWCASTLE.

[Harl. MSS. No. 4955, fol. 204.]

" My Noble and most honor'd Lord,

" I myself being no substance, am fain to
" trouble you with shadows, or (what is less) an
" Apologue or Fable in a dream. I being strucken
" with the Palsy in the year 1628, had by Sir
" Thomas Badger some few months since a Fox
" sent me for a present, which creature by hand-
" ling I endeavoured to make tame, as well for
" the abating of my disease as the delight I took
" in speculation of his nature. It happened this
" present year, 1631, and this very week, being
" the week ushering Christmas, and this Tuesday
" morning in a dream (and morning dreams are
" truest), to have one of my servants come up to
" my bedside, and tell me, ' Master, Master, the
" ' Fox speaks !' Whereat (me thought) I started,
" and troubled went down into the yard to wit-
" ness the wonder. There I found my Reynard,
" in his tenement—the Tub I had hired for him

" —cynically expressing his own lot to be con-
" demned to the house of a Poet, where nothing
" was to be seen but the bare walls, and not any-
" thing heard but the noise of a saw, dividing
" billets all the day long, more to keep the family
" in exercise than to comfort any person there with
" fire, save the paralytick master; and went on
" in this way, as the Fox seemed the better
" Fabler of the two. I, his master, began to
" give him good words and stroke him, but Rey-
" nard, barking, told me those would not do, I
" must give him meat. I angry called him stink-
" ing vermin. He replied, 'Look into your cel-
" 'lar, which is your larder too, you'll find a worse
" 'vermin there.' When presently, calling for a
" light, me thought I went down and found all
" the floor turned up, as if a colony of moles had
" been there, or an army of Salt-petre men.
" Whereupon I sent presently into Tuttle Street
" for the King's most excellent Mole-catcher to
" relieve me and hunt them. But he, when he
" came and viewed the place, and had well marked
" the earth turned up, took a handfull, smelt it,
" and said, 'Master, it is not in my power to de-
" 'stroy this vermin; the King, or some good man
" 'of a Noble Nature, must help you. This kind
" 'of Mole is called a WANT, which will destroy

"'you and your family if you prevent not the
"'working of it in time. And therefore God
"'keep you and send you health.'

"The interpretation both of the Fable and
"dream is, that I waking do find WANT the worst
"and most working vermin in a house; and
"therefore my noble Lord, and next the King
"my best patron, I am necessitated to tell it you.
"I am not so impudent to borrow any sum of
"your lordship, for I have no faculty to pay; but
"my needs are such, and so urging, as I do beg
"what your bounty can give me in the name of
"Good Letters, and the bond of an ever grateful
"and acknowledging servant.

"To your honour,

"BEN JONSON.

" *Westminster*, 20mo *Dec^{bris}*, 1631.

"Yesterday the barbarous Court of Aldermen
"have withdrawn their Chandlerly Pension for
"Verjuice and Mustard, 33^{li} 6 8."

Cardinal BENTIVOGLIO, whose rank, learning,
and talents rendered him one of the chief ornaments of the age in which he lived, sank, in his
old age, into a condition of the most distressing
poverty. His palace was sacrificed for the satisfaction of clamorous creditors, and he died pos-

sessed of nothing beyond the noble reputation which no evil destiny could wrench from him.

BAKER, the historian, might not claim the highest credit of a writer of his class, but his labours are certainly not deserving of the low estimate too often expressed in regard to their merits. Certain it is that he was neglected, and suffered to languish in great poverty. He has had many detractors, and not a few of them were unworthy to hold an opinion on any subject he handled.

The late poet, Rogers, possessed the identical receipt which showed that our most sublime poem, '*Paradise Lost*,' was sold for the wretched sum of fifteen pounds by its immortal author, who was too poor to make any arrangement for printing it on his own account.

We hardly dare trust our indignant pen to the mortifying task of recording in this melancholy list of sufferers the venerated name of the "Prince of English Satirists"—the inimitable author of '*Hudibras*,' whose life was one prolonged scene of shifting dependence and broken hopes—an uninterrupted series of accumulating disappointments. While the most worthless of all ignoble princes was absorbed in profligate revelry, he could yet gratify his keen relish for the charms of BUTLER's unrivalled wit and humour, and apply to the needs and uses of his daily life the sprightly aphorisms of the poet's wisdom, regardless of the neglected source of this borrowed display. Was there a concealed sarcasm in Kneller's everlasting choice of a Roman habit in the portraits of this abject monarch, as adapted to render more close the resemblance which he bore to the character of Tiberius?

THOMAS OTWAY, in whose dramatic writings are to be found some of the finest specimens of impassioned poetry embodied in our language, died at an obscure tavern in the Minories, while eagerly swallowing a roll which charity had bestowed to quell the pangs of hunger. Indigence, care, and despondency brought him to an untimely grave, in his thirty-fourth year. Thus perished out of a nation's diadem the sweetest pearl that ever shed a softened radiance on the brow of sovereignty; or, to change our metaphor for one of more popular import, thus closed for ever a glorious mine of unmeted wealth, when the grave received that early and illustrious victim.

A mean cottage in the suburbs of Paris, and a chronic state of pecuniary embarrassment, presented the scene and circumstances which surrounded the charming writer LE SAGE. From this miserable abode of want and obscurity came forth those delicious and wonderful romances that have bewitched readers of every clime and class. No comfort, no ease, no enjoyment of even temporary relief from the galling pressure of destitution, was permitted to gladden the existence of one of the world's most distinguished literary benefactors.

In a small cottage in a poor village, condemned to perpetual labour as a "literary hack," denied the satisfaction of preparing his contributions to the press with the care alone consistent with hours of permitted leisure, existed—not lived—the distinguished French poet DE RYER, whose works, while indicating the rapidity with which they were written, show most painfully how much might have been expected from their author under the favouring auspices of a brighter destiny. His heroic verses, we are told, were purchased by his bookseller at the paltry rate of 100 sols the 100 lines, and the smaller ones for 50 sols.

PAUL COLOMIES, a distinguished French writer, fell a victim to poverty, sorrow, and disease, and at his death added another name to the Appendix of Pierius Valerianus's treatise "*De Infelicitate Literatorum*," On the Miseries of Learned Men.

DRYDEN—*Claud Halero's* "Glorious John"— received for 10,000 immortal verses, from the clever trader Tonson, not quite £300, as is proved by the agreement which has been published. After a life of prolonged literary splendour, this great man died in complete poverty, his very remains denied a grave by a malevolent creditor, whose hostility had to be bought off by some charitable person.

Honest GEORGE FARQUHAR! thy soul of fire was too early withdrawn from the sphere which it irradiated; and thy gleams of wit (alas for genius!) were too often overshadowed with the dark clouds of pecuniary distress!

THOMAS D'URFEY, more generally spoken of by the familiar name of TOM, wrote many dramatic pieces, which were well received by the public, but his greatest reputation was derived from his songs, satires, and irregular odes. His wit and facetious manners caused him to be familiarly noticed by that appreciative monarch Charles the Second, whose customary liberality to literary talent struggling with distress was evidenced in the case of "poor TOM," whom his merry Majesty left to struggle on as best he might; and the poor fellow, slowly sinking under ever-increasing embarrassments, died at length in extreme poverty. How small a pension would have saved him from this wretched fate !

Died, in poverty, of a broken heart, a victim of base ingratitude, NICHOLAS AMHURST, a profes-sional writer, who was buried at the charge of his worthy printer, Richard Francklin, after a long literary career, during which he had actively and often successfully opposed the Walpole ad-ministration. Such is the assured fate of all who indulge the promptings of a generous and patriotic spirit. The work is done—done well—but who is responsible for the remuneration due to the workman's toil ? He must look to himself as his only employer. Such is the silent but most eloquent decree of public opinion on the question, a further illustration, if wanted, of the truth of Zeno's axiom, that " virtue is its own reward."

A life of penury and wretchedness concluded in a jail at Bristol—his burial expenses defrayed by the humane jailer—gives to the memory of RICHARD SAVAGE a pointed moral. That hideous old fiend in female attire, the Countess of Mac-clesfield, his unnatural mother, rises before our disturbed vision as we cast our sympathizing glance upon the poor wasted corpse of her hapless son—of that son rescued at last, by the friendly aid of Death, from a scene of life-long suffering.

He had "troops of friends," who have preached to the world of the disregard of the common maxims of life of the unhappy sufferer, without reflecting, or, if they did reflect, without acknowledging, that the prudence of which they boasted as their own possession, was a guest of a different quality to those "wingèd visitors" that throng the palace-halls of the soul's Elysium, as existing in the rapt bosom of the poet, and illuminated by the splendour of divine genius. The present remark applies generally to the accusations brought by worldly-minded calculators against the infirmity of imaginative natures. No sympathy can possibly exist between such characters. Seekers of wealth have their gaze ever bent earthward; they cannot understand the "divine madness" of the bard of lofty inspiration—of the dreamer of those trancing, soul-enthralling mysteries, "half thought, half vision."

Though SAVAGE was not a poet of this exalted grade, he had still, however, a large share of the poetic temperament, and enjoyed his banquets of Parnassus, alternately with others of a more sensuous kind, as is the wont of men of strong passions, such as poets are by nature created, as the very source of their inspiration. SAVAGE has been branded by his assumed "benefactors"

with the vices of intemperance and ingratitude ;
and so respectable in the " eyes of the world "
are these charity-devoted worthies, that we cannot but believe in the truth of their combined
representations; but we must ask the question
whether much of that " intemperance " was not
due to their own ill-timed and exaggerated reproofs and contumely; and whether some share
of that " ingratitude " was not too often the
natural—nay, the inevitable feeling inspired by
their perpetual trumpetings, kettle-drummings,
and gong-beatings in public laudation of their own
supreme virtues in *alms-giving*. We never yet
heard men or women much abused that we were not
inclined to think the better of them.   Where, we
ask, were the boasted friends and admirers of
the unfortunate bard when, for the mean sum of
ten pounds, he was compelled to sell the copyright
of his best poem, " *The Wanderer*," on which he
had expended the lavish labour of years ?

SAMUEL BOYSE, the author of the well-known
poem on the " *Deity*," whose merit has been
highly estimated by the most judicious critics,
was literally starved to death.   His body was
found, lying in a wretched garret, near Shoe
Lane, London, partially covered with a ragged
blanket, fastened over the shoulders with a

G

skewer, and—touching fact!—his pen was re-
maining in his hand, stiffened by death! He
was buried at the expense of the parish. Be it
remembered that in that hour of consummated
misery—in that last stage of the poet's career
of ignominious want—many thousands of low-
thoughted, sensual beings, with scarcely more of
the intellectual nature than served to keep their
bodies from putrefaction, were rioting amidst the
costliest superfluities of life.

THOMAS CHATTERTON, name most prominently
associated with the martyrdom of genius! CHAT-
TERTON, the boy-critic, the self-formed scholar,
the born poet, from whose facile and elastic pen
might have been surely expected one of the
loftiest productions of epic design, and whose
memory would have been enrolled amid the
proudest records of his country's greatness. Cut
off, while yet in the bloom of youth, from every
pleasurable source of feeling, haunted by fears
of impending starvation, a prey to the direful
promptings of the demon despair, he was goaded
to self-destruction; while a crowd of imbecile
and worthless creatures, of the type of my Lord
Orford, lisped their vapid and unfelt regrets at
his untimely fate, in such exclamations as:—
" Lord! how monstrous shocking! What would

the wretched, sinful fellow have wished for?" Answer:—"*Could* it have been the luxury of a little *bread* to his water?"

Many a single stanza from the pen of CHATTERTON was worth tons of such mawkish trash as the *belauded* and be-*lorded* Walpole scribbled, as in open contempt for his readers' intellect. Sad reflection! that that small sordid insect should still flap its tiny wing in all the pride of its gilded insignificance, while the stately eagle of empyrean descent should droop its princely crest and ethereal pinion amid the solitary desolation of the wilderness!

Such a genius as CHATTERTON'S appears not above once in many centuries. It was not for a mind like that of Horatio *Tad*pole (we blush for this involuntary, maladroit inaccuracy of our trippant—not flippant pen), we mean *Wal*pole, to appreciate the extraordinary instance of mental grandeur that was revealed in the glory of the "Bard of Severn." There could be no sympathetic reverberation in a breast like *his*.

Poor OLIVER GOLDSMITH! Simple, honest, humane, and generous—witty, learned, versatile, laborious—endowed with every quality for worldly success in abundance, except the guiding quality of discretion. The frequent associate of high-

born and influential men, to whose patronizing
notice he was recommended by the reputation of
successful authorship, this unfortunate writer was
often without the humble means of discharging
his laundress's score. Plentiful, indeed, were the
sarcasms heaped upon his "vanity" and "extravagance," by the wretched souls who affected to
love him, who, without a thousandth part of his
genius and scholarship, thought that they gave,
rather than received honour, in admitting him
to their misplaced intimacy. The old adage,
"Gold can gild a rotten stick, and dirt sully an
ingot," well applies to cases like this.

Dr. SAMUEL JOHNSON, the "Great Moralist,"
the "Leviathan of Literature," during the greater
part of his long career, led a poor and mean life,
haunted with constantly growing cares and embarrassments, straining under a load of mental
toil that would have bowed a less powerful moral
athlete to the dust. As his fame extended, his
circle of professing personal admirers also became enlarged; he was banqueted with smiles
of adulation, and exaggerated expressions of
reverence and regard; but influential as some of
these associates doubtless were, he appears to
have owed nothing to their boasted friendship,
and but for the timely grant of a royal pension

of £300 per annum, his later years would have
certainly been exposed to the indignity of pecuniary distress. This distinguished man never
appears to ourselves in so depreciated a point of
view, as when surrounded by the many small
spirits of the "Langton" class, whose names
have been so impertinently connected with his
memory. These petty pretenders to literary
taste, whose persons became known to the world
through his indulgent tolerance of their pygmy
insignificance, seem to have owed their place in
his regard to the craving, natural to those of
high parts and studious application, for opportunities of ventilating ideas, in reference to the
objects of their present researches or speculations,
—a species of talking aloud to themselves, which
may occasionally serve to promote the more rapid
operations of the mind.

The celebrated French writer, MARMONTEL, died
in a state bordering on want, in a little cottage
situate in an obscure village. A sad doom for a
man, whose long career of literary success had
given promise of a more cheerful retirement in
the decline of life, since the extent of reverses is
in a correspondent ratio with the degree of affluence and enjoyment once possessed.

ROBERT BURNS, a poet by nature's own tran-

scendent ordination! Born in the deepest obscurity, debarred any advantage arising from
scholastic culture, he nevertheless indulged the
early promptings of an inborn genius, and put
forth such proofs of high superiority above the
laboured productions of more lofty pretenders to
the palm of Parnassian inspiration, that the eyes
of the astonished public were irresistibly drawn
to the rude hut in which the "Ayrshire plough-
man" kindled the torch of a destined immortality. The learned commended; the nobles
repeated the praises of the learned; fair dames
of the highest quality warbled the rustic com-
poser's soul-wrought lays, and loaded him with
sugared compliments. Yet Scotland's dukes and
duchesses could think of no higher secular employment, for the poet's fulfilment, than the
office of a gauger or exciseman; the poor deluded
expectant awoke from his brief dream of laureated
triumphs, to find himself cut off from all sympathy with his crowds of admirers in high places.
Chained, as it were, to a lower sphere of repulsive
vulgarity, exposed to the cares and privations of
penury, humiliated and self-loathing, he sank,
gradually but surely, into the depths of dissipa-
tion, distress, and despair. Never fell a darker
blot upon the vaunted national shield of Scotland,

than when the immortal author of " Bruce's Address to his Army," the " Cottager's Saturday Night," and other unrivalled compositions, welcomed the untimely aid of death as a release from suffering, a prey to destitution and neglect.

GILBERT WAKEFIELD, whose character, in many respects, resembled that of the philosophers of antiquity, a man possessed of the deepest learning, of a lofty independence of mind, and of a spirit of indomitable energy and perseverance under difficulties, lived a melancholy life of constant embarrassment and unsuccessful exertion, uncheered by a single gleam of substantial sympathy, though beset with admiring correspondents among the minions of rank and fortune, who could easily have procured for him that moderate advancement, which his simple and manly nature would have preferred to the pride of higher station. He sank at length, the victim of political persecution, brought on, perhaps, by a misguided course of vain ambition, which led him to imperil his liberty, sacrifice his worldly prospects, and alienate many of his best friends, for the empty indulgence of the pride of patriotic martyrdom. The proverb of " *Anagyrum commovere*," signifying the bringing of misfortunes upon one's self, well applies to this most imprudent portion of an honourable life.

THOMAS DERMODY, born with talents of the most extraordinary brilliancy, and whose acquirements were as rare as his natural endowments, adds another and most prominent example of the misery too often attendant upon the possession of elevated intellect. Driven to excess and to low habits by the abject state of dependence and distress which accompanied the whole of his life, bound down by the chains of necessity to a lot which appeared irredeemably evil, he drank to drown the maddening taunts of self-contempt provoked and intensified, as they too often were, by the cold mockery of affected Mæcenases; heartless wretches, who glorified themselves and each other while only aping the appearance of true patronage. These sordid pretenders marked with habitual insult their petty donations, heaping reproofs upon his alleged misconduct at the moment of their sham relief.

Poor DERMODY died of consumption, in a wretched hovel at Sydenham, Kent, released, at length, from his many " constant patrons," whose whinings in self-eulogy, and whose barkings in condemnation of the poet's reckless improvidence and ingratitude, were happily unheard by the sad victim of a life's unchanging misery.

Brief, but illustrious, was the career of HENRY

KIRKE WHITE, who fell a martyr to the exertions of a mind worn out by too persevering study. Equally distinguished by his piety, attainments, and inherent genius, his career may be cited as a melancholy warning to the few ardent spirits that, like his own, see but the tempting goal of their praiseworthy ambition, not asking themselves whether their *viaticum* be proportioned to the length of their pilgrimage. Talents exhausted by fruitless toil, acquirements made but to be speedily buried in the tomb, lost to the world and to themselves, exhibit, in his instance, a most memorable and emphatic lesson. But his name survives, an undying monument of the united qualities of the poet, the scholar, and the Christian. On that monument, a tributary wreath, culled by the hand of a fellow-native of the "old forest town" of Nottingham, is now laid, with a solemn affirmatory response to the just observation of a talented contemporary and personal friend of the writer, in his essay '*On the Genius of Nottinghamshire.*' "How little could the proud Duchess of Devonshire have dreamt that she was very near silencing for ever those Trent-side warblings of that pale and lonely boy, who was so soon to draw pilgrims across the Atlantic, to visit the spots which his Muse had

invested with thrilling interest; so soon to exert
an influence on the mind of his native town and
county, and so soon to acquire a name which
should be remembered when the proud Duchess
of Devonshire should be forgotten!"

RICHARD BRINSLEY SHERIDAN, gives another
name to posterity, associated with the evils that
beset the course of the possessor of lofty talents.
Such, alas! is too often the man for whom misfortune reserves her darkest frowns. From his
nature incapable of sordid consideration, slow in
the pursuit of mercenary advantage, open to im-
pressions of intellectual enjoyment that lead the
mind from the common paths of worldly interest,
he is too apt to neglect the financial considerations
that operate as a check to the less discursive
habits of individuals of commonplace ideas.

This distinguished man has been accused, by a
host of glib-tongued censors, of incurring debt
without probable means of payment; but how
difficult a question it is to decide what is a reason-
able expectation of being able to discharge such
claims! "In such cases," suggests an acute
logician, whose argument does honour to his
heart as well as his understanding, "we must
enter into the man's mind, estimate his powers
of hopefulness, make allowance for differences of

temperament, take into consideration, too, the ability or non-ability to calculate the chances of success. Some men will indulge expectations, and sometimes realize them, which others scout as ridiculous."

We are no apologists for extravagance and vice. But we are not of the number of those who expect from the enthusiasm of the man of refined taste and elevated genius the calculating coolness and measured parsimony of the illiterate boor whose nature excludes an idea of spiritual luxury. The temperament of the man of wit and humorous vivacity essentially differs from that of the everlasting thinker in prose. The errors of a man of genius are usually less offensive than those of his moralizing critics. It has been well observed that virtue and vice have as much resemblance, when they reach their extremest points, as light and fire. Good motives are not always crowned with success, and misfortune is apt to incur blame. The strokes of misfortune demand our pity for the sufferer. It is a beautiful saying that misery is sacred. " *Res est sacra, miser.*" To vulgar natures such a sentiment may appear absurd. We envy not their feelings or their judgment. It were useless to preach such a truth in certain ears ; as useless, indeed, as to apply the lash of satire or invective. As Shake-speare says, "Your dull ass will not mend his pace by beating."

With all his vices or faults, whatever they were, we would gladly look upon another SHERIDAN.

A few years ago, the 'Post' recorded the death of a French Chatterton : — "In the hospital, where, melancholy to relate, die one-third of the population of the Parisian Babylon, a few days since, expired one of the most remarkable poets of France. HÉGÉSIPPE NOREAU, a young and obscure journeyman printer, astonished the literary world of Paris by publishing a poem called 'Mysotis,' replete with that intensity of feeling and warmth of imagination which can alone soar above a dark destiny. His admirers were numerous, and many an empty-handed Mæcenas smiled upon him his hollow patronage. But if the praise of his contemporaries yielded to him that 'feast of the soul' which most of all he prized, it was barren of that sustenance of the body, which most he needed. For more than two years he proudly and silently struggled with that devouring domestic wolf, want, until at last he fell a prey to disease. Then were opened to him the doors of the hospital—that last refuge of the poor of all classes in France, the chosen land of human vicissitude. The literary world of Paris heard of his last trials and of his death with surprise, not unmingled with shame and remorse. National vanity took alarm, and the poet who could not obtain in his lifetime the rations of a common soldier, after death received the honours of a prince. His body, saved from the scalpel of the anatomist, has been embalmed, and his features, resting at last in death, moulded by the statuary for the sculptor." He was interred with great funeral pomp at Père la Chaise.

We append half-a-dozen samples of more liberal treatment accorded to distinguished men of letters in modern times.

The modesty of high merit is beautifully illustrated in the instance of JOHN WESSEL, of Groeningen, one of the most learned men of the age of Sixtus IV. That Pope sent for him, and said, " Son, ask of us what you will ; nothing shall be refused that becomes our character to bestow and your condition to receive." " Most holy father," said he, " my generous patron, I shall not be troublesome to your Holiness. You know that I never sought after great things. The only favour I have to beg is that you would give me, out of your Vatican library, a Greek and a Hebrew Bible." " You shall have them," said Sixtus,

" but what a simple man are you! Why do you
not ask a bishopric?" Wessel replied, " Because
I do not want one." Dr. Jortin, from whose en-
tertaining pages we quote this anecdote, observes,
" The happier man was he; happier than they
who would give all the Bibles in the Vatican, if
they had them to give, for a bishopric."

LEO X. was both a genius and a protector of
men of talent. His court was an academy.

PAULUS JOVIUS, a celebrated historian, was
made Bishop of Nocera, and enjoyed a consider-
able pension from this monarch.

Charles V. sent ARETIN a chain of gold worth a
hundred ducats. "A very small present this,"
observed the satirist, " considering the Emperor's
late enormous follies."

MICHAEL ANGELO RICCI, one of the greatest
geometricians of his time, was offered a Cardinal's
hat by Pope Innocent the Eleventh, an honour
which his modesty led him to refuse.

FERDOUS, a Persian historian in verse, received
from the king under whose reign he lived, a piece
of gold for every distich his work contained. The
number was 60,000.

THE END.

www.ingramcontent.com/pod-product-compliance
Lightning Source LLC
Chambersburg PA
CBHW022146020726
47496CB00008B/2575